The Creighton Lecture in History 1972

The
Young Wellington
in India

C. H. PHILIPS
M.A., PH.D., D.LITT., LL.D.

Vice-Chancellor of the University of London
Director of the School of Oriental and African Studies

UNIVERSITY OF LONDON
THE ATHLONE PRESS
1973

Published by
THE ATHLONE PRESS
UNIVERSITY OF LONDON
at 4 Gower Street, London WC1

Distributed by Tiptree Book Services Ltd
Tiptree, Essex

U.S.A. and Canada
Humanities Press Inc
New York

0 485 14120 5

Printed in Great Britain by
H. E. WARNE LTD, LONDON AND ST. AUSTELL

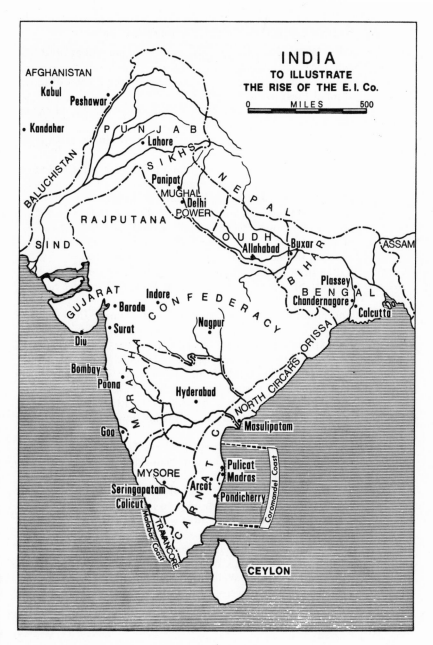

INDIA
TO ILLUSTRATE
THE RISE OF THE E. I. Co.

0   MILES   500

AFGHANISTAN

Kabul

Peshawar

Kandahar

BALUCHISTAN

PUNJAB

Lahore

SIKHS

Panipat

MUGHAL
POWER

Delhi

NEPAL

RAJPUTANA

OUDH

Allahabad

Buxar

ASSAM

SIND

BIHAR

Plassey

BENGAL

Chandernagore

Calcutta

GUJARAT

Indore

CONFEDERACY

Baroda

Surat

Diu

Nagpur

NORTH CIRCARS

ORISSA

Bombay

Poona

MARATHA

Hyderabad

Goa

Masulipatam

MYSORE

CARNATIC

Pulicat

Madras

Coromandel Coast

Seringapatam

Arcot

Pondicherry

Calicut

Malabar Coast

TRAVANCORE

CEYLON

1

This lecture was illustrated by the following slides:

1. Arthur Wellesley (1795) by Hoppner from a portrait at Stratfield Saye.
2. Arthur Wellesley (1804) by Robert Home from a portrait in the National Portrait Gallery.
3. Arthur Wellesley (1804) from a miniature by an unknown artist in the National Portrait Gallery, shown on the cover.
4. Richard Wellesley from a painting by Robert Home, 1804, India Office Library.
5. Henry Wellesley by Hoppner from a portrait at Stratfield Saye.
6. Fort William at Bengal from an engraving by Van der Gucht.
7. Calcutta, European houses, by Henry Salt, 1809.
8. Calcutta, Writers' Buildings, by J. B. Fraser, 1824.
9. Calcutta, Esplanade Row, by J. B. Fraser, 1824.
10. Calcutta, Views of Government House by J. B. Fraser, 1824.
11. Calcutta, Barrackpore House, by J. B. Fraser, 1824.
12. Madras from the sea, from *The European Magazine*, 1783.
13. Old Fort St. George, Madras, from Daniell's *Oriental Scenery*, I.O.L.
14. Panorama roll of the British army on the march, I.O.L.
15. Portrait of Tipu Sultan, ruler of Mysore, I.O.L.
16. Seringapatam from *Memories of Madras* (1905), C. Lawson.
17. Seringapatam from a drawing by R. H. Colebrooke, I.O.L.
18. Sketch of Sultanpettah from the journal of Captain Colin Mackenzie in the British Museum, Add. Mss. 13663, f.77.
19. The Maratha army from a drawing in the I.O.L.
20. Seevendrug in Mysore from a drawing by R. H. Colebrooke, I.O.L.
21. Gawilghur from a drawing by Meadows Taylor, I.O.L.
22. Maratha camp scene by Captain Johnson, I.O.L.
23. Maratha hill fort by Captain Johnson, I.O.L.
24. Sketch of the battle of Assaye, M. Elphinstone from the *Life* by R. H. Colebrooke, shown on p.29 in the text.
25. Battle of Assaye from Dr Syntax's *Wars of Wellington* (1819) in the British Museum.
26. Two contemporary maps of Mysore at the close of the eighteenth century; also two maps of India in 1795 and 1805. By kind permission of Mr Jac Weller diagrams of the battles of Sultanpettah and Assaye were used from his *Wellington in India* (1972), and part of the former appears in the text, p.16.

THE YOUNG WELLINGTON IN INDIA

It was through adversity in early life, through harsh trial and error, that the young Wellington came to know himself; and it was but slowly in the seven long years in India that there emerged through challenge and response, defeat and victory, the confident, self-contained, famous commander of armies and ruler of men. Desperately unhappy and frustrated up to the time in 1796 when, at the age of twenty-seven, he left Britain for India, we cannot describe him better in early life than by recalling the well known lines of Alexander Pope:

> He hangs between; in doubt to act or rest;
> In doubt to deem himself a god or beast;
> In doubt his mind or body to prefer;
> Chaos of thought and passions all confused;
> Still by himself abused or disabused.

Without some understanding of the significance of these early experiences of Arthur Wellesley—Wellington as he later became—we cannot appreciate the extent of the change which India produced in him, and I must therefore by way of introduction say something about this.

But this lecture essentially deals with the vast and rapid transformation brought about in India by Arthur and his elder brother, Richard, who between them created the high point of British imperial conquest, the most splendid and convincing example in our history of a government autocratic and imperial in the best sense of the words. In this process, I seek to explain their critical relationship, which was to close with the dissolution of the brilliant Richard and the making, through victory and defeat, of the mature Arthur. They represented two philosophies of conquest, a theme to which I will return in conclusion.

3

The subject is buried by the weight and variety of contemporary evidence; and subsequently the biographers have been active, but one characteristic of the latter, understandably enough, is that they have rarely looked as closely and extensively into the British-Indian material as into the European. So there is still an opportunity to say something fresh.

Arthur was the third eldest son in a family of five brothers and two sisters. The family was Anglo-Irish, newly elevated into the upper ranks of that dominant English minority which, in the face of an alien Irish population, dramatised its ambitions and fears in the careless, exotic, social masquerade of Dublin Castle. Later in India the Wellesley brothers were to find this kind of social pattern strangely familiar, and not uncomfortable. The family's newly-won status was soon threatened for the father, more devoted to music than management, allowed the family fortunes to be dissipated, and, then at the point of bankruptcy, inconveniently died, leaving his young wife, Anne, reputedly 'deficient of education', to bring up the boys.

The mother's favourite son, Richard—later to become Governor-General of India—the eldest and then only twenty, with typical easy confidence, took the family in hand. Possessing great intellectual gifts, he had whilst at Eton and Christ Church become the talk of London, toasted by Garrick, as the first classical scholar of his day. Admired by William Pitt and Grenville, pushed on by the Duke of Buckingham, and with boundless ambition, he slipped smoothly into the House of Commons and a junior lordship at the Treasury, and from this vantage point actively set about managing the future for himself and for the rest of the family.

Arthur, nine years his junior, and Henry even younger still, followed him to Eton, but Arthur was everything that Richard was not and that Richard deplored: idle, dreamy, shy, and dejected. He could make little of Eton and, outshone by Richard's brilliance and Henry's cleverness, was removed after two years to give his younger brothers a better chance. He was then sent for twelve months to Brussels to a finishing school—vaguely military in disposition—Richard and his mother having reached the conclusion that he was idle, awkward, and 'food for powder and nothing more'.

The mother's feelings for Arthur were said by a close friend to be 'not far removed from aversion' and although within a family struggling to make its way family loyalty remained strong, Arthur, despite what some recent biographers have suggested, disliked her, and moreover resented Richard's control and manner. Between Arthur and his younger brother, Henry, there was an easier relationship, but the general coolness of the family towards Arthur can be inferred from the fact that when later he went to India no one bothered to write to him for over a year, and that Arthur could bitterly say that 'he was a bad judge of the pain a man feels upon parting from his family'.

So at eighteen Arthur went into the army, the cost of his commission being borrowed for the purpose. 'What commission is a matter of indifference to me,' said Richard, 'provided he gets it soon'.

For the next nine years, with a short, unnerving interlude in the Flanders campaign of 1794, after the outbreak of war with revolutionary France Arthur spent much of his time in London and Dublin, savouring the superior brothels of Seymour Street, near Hyde Park in London, and the gaming tables of Dublin, the money meanwhile somehow being raised to buy him promotion to a Lieut.-Colonelcy of the 33rd Regiment. In Dublin although absorbed in the dissipation and 'the wheeling and dealing' of the Castle, he met and fell deeply in love with Kitty Pakenham, daughter of Lord Longford. He courted her, and sought her hand in marriage, only to be crushingly rejected by the family for want of prospects.

This blow to his pride, associated with a humiliating failure to get even a minor place in Irish Government, shook him into an anxious reappraisal of his life. He burnt his favourite fiddle, symbol of his father's failure, and took refuge in the hard reality of regimental accounts, but his chronic frustration brought on a debilitating fever, I suppose a kind of psychosomatic illness, which as we shall see was later to recur at several crises in his life in India.

From the depths of despair he found relief and fresh hope when his Regiment was put on orders for posting overseas. Recovering quickly, he gathered his possessions and gladly took ship for the Cape and Calcutta in June, 1796, there to join the small army which was charged with the defence of the British East India Company's territories in India.

Ever afterwards throughout his long life he maintained a grim reticence about these early years. Emotionally deprived, overshadowed by and resentful of his lofty brother, half-educated, entangled in debt, failing to find family affection, love or a vocation, he had at least in sickness, despair and confusion turned to examine himself. 'Know then thyself', Alexander Pope had declared, but for Arthur the process demanded the abandonment of his old life and the pursuit of a new career, as it happened in India.

For quiet reflection about himself and his future there was ample time on the voyage out—usually four to five months, but on this occasion nine tedious months; time, too, for serious reading, and before leaving London he had provided himself with £50-worth of new books. They tell us something about him and his mood. Apart from the accepted tracts and histories of India, Rennell's *Maps*, the hopeful Arabic and Persian grammars, the Oriental phrase book, there were the soldier's tools of trade, Dundas's drill and army training manuals, and on the art of war, Frederick the Great, Marshal Saxe, Dumourier, and Caesar's *Commentaries*—in Latin—with a Latin dictionary; sad comment on his time at Eton! Plutarch's *Lives* in English, well read, and influential as we shall later see. For law, he took Blackstone; for economics, Adam Smith; for philosophy, Locke; for theology, Paley; for politics, Bolingbroke; and Hume and Robertson for history. For lighter reading, there were twenty four volumes of the sardonic Irishman, Swift; Rousseau's *Nouvelle Héloise*, and in sharp contrast some volumes of the sceptical Voltaire. For a military man it was a sizable, surprisingly wide-ranging collection, almost all for use. A library which for one so inclined could help to make a full and exact man.

But all was not reading. With his strong face and muscular build—he was about 5′ 9″ tall—clear, cool, blue eyes, quick speech and ready laughter, he was attractive to the ladies, particularly to two young sisters, one of whom, Henrietta, caught his fancy with her 'pretty little figure and lovely neck'. And there was hard drinking in his officers' mess, so notorious, that when at last they got ashore at Calcutta, they were at once invited into the rip-roaring circle of William Hickey.

Anglo-Indian society at this time, that is largely in the towns of Calcutta, Madras and Bombay, was a minute frontier society —numbering no more than 25,000 Europeans, civil and military, perched on the fringe of the vast, complex life of India. There were about a thousand Europeans continuously in Calcutta, not more than a hundred of whom were women, living in the midst of 60,000 Indians spread out along five miles of the steamy, broad and muddy river Hugli. In Madras, there were half this number of Europeans and in Bombay about a quarter.

Ever since Clive's conquests thirty years earlier the East India Company had controlled the two large provinces of Bengal and Madras, their presence resented by powerful neighbours, who apparently had only to agree among themselves to drive them out. These Anglo-Indian societies were cosmopolitan, exotic, masculine and dissipated; life was nasty and short, and meanwhile there was money to be made and power to be won. Death, never far away, for one in three died soon after arrival, was utterly unaccountable. They either gaily and hard-heartedly defied disease and the climate with a full-bodied claret (and a natural immunity) or soon passed quietly beneath a sombre tombstone in the local graveyard.

One sufferer, Sir John Lloyd, was given up by his doctor, who declared, 'He cannot survive two hours more'. And the coffin bearer party was summoned. But the patient, we are told, 'was indebted to claret for his very unexpected recovery; during the last week of the disease we poured down his throat,' said the doctor, 'from three to four bottles of that generous beverage every twenty-four hours; and with extraordinary effect.'

7

In pursuit of his new career Arthur did not much like what he saw. 'Taking the natives and the climate together,' he said, 'India is a miserable country to live in, and a man well deserves some of the wealth which is sometimes brought him.' Still relatively junior in rank, his chances of promotion and wealth seemed slim, and a pacifically inclined Company's government living in the shadow of William Pitt's India Act, which forbade 'schemes of conquest', offered little hope of action.

At this juncture his prospects were totally transformed by the news that his brilliant elder brother, Richard, with the full support of William Pitt and Henry Dundas and the British wartime cabinet was coming out as the next Governor-General of British India, bringing the younger brother, Henry, with him as private secretary. In Richard's view it was 'the most distinguished situation in the British Empire after that of Prime Minister of England' and by far the most lucrative, carrying at least £25,000 a year with emoluments.

The fortunes of the family thus seemed assured, and the Colonel brother of the Governor-General could hopefully begin to plan a career. Seemingly, his conversion is complete and at a stroke William Hickey's world is rejected, and without self-consciousness Arthur can advise the younger Henry:

I know but one receipt for good health in this country, and that is to live moderately, to drink little or no wine, to exercise, to keep the mind employed, and, if possible, to keep in good humour with the world. The last is the most difficult.

Richard Wellesley, like Lord Curzon later, had early announced that India politically was of interest to him only if he could make his mark there before he was forty. He was in fact thirty-eight and he came singlemindedly to establish the British as the arbiters of an Indian empire in which he would be the prime mover. His abilities were unquestionable, his vision and moral courage great, he had the insight to pierce directly to the heart of political problems, and the capacity to inspire men and draw the best out of them. He turned a society of merchants into a great empire, the provincial town of Calcutta into a ruling metropolis. Although physically small and slight, he could bend strong men to his own way. As we can see from his dark, piercing gaze he could summon an intense force of nervous and creative energy, which however left him totally exhausted, so that he was apt to pass easily from the heights to the depths, in which increasingly during his Indian service he suffered breakdown. In fact, India quite broke him down, and afterwards he was never the same man.

He was a strange man who made enemies freely and easily, and provoked the most extreme judgments on his character and merits. On the one side, there is Croker's disparaging 'brilliant incapacity' and Curzon's 'inordinate vanity in high places'; on the other P. E. Roberts's 'ruler of wonderful achievement and glorious capacity'. And the truth lies not midway between these extremes but in both of them. Richard was great and small, noble and petty, a brilliant empire-builder and yet ridiculous in his conceits, a womanizer who could blacken his eyebrows, whiten his forehead and cry endlessly and piteously for a dukedom. There was a total lack of proportion between his achievement and his personality. By comparison, Arthur, now fast growing into manhood, appears in his Indian phase as consistent, balanced and all of a piece. In India Richard touched the rainbow, and never did so again.

One explanation, which is convincing, is that he was never again in such close co-operation with Arthur, and with so brilliant a band of subordinates, about whom I will speak in a moment. Nevertheless, from the combination of the elder brother's soaring imagination and ambition, and comprehensive grasp in the realm of political policy, and the younger's magnificent balance of common sense, sanity and tolerance in the world of reality, with the inherent antagonisms and temperamental clashes smoothed away by Henry, a diplomatic secretary if ever there was one, there was forged a superbly efficient instrument for the task of conquering and governing men. Together in India they became a formidable trio, the most famous brothers of their generation.

Within seven years, in material additions to Britain, they swept away the empire of Mysore in the south, occupied

9

Hyderabad in the centre, took over the Carnatic, Tanjore and Surat on the coasts, occupied the north-west area beyond Bengal, and brought the Marathas of western India to acknowledge British paramountcy.

Richard sailed from England in one of the darkest years of her history. Disaster at the hands of the French revolutionary forces everywhere attended her armies and navy. With Pitt and his inner circle he watched the revolution in France begin to stir all Europe. In fear that Britain might be submerged, they worked themselves into a frenzy of patriotism against Jacobinism—a term as widely and loosely used and as feared as Communism in our own day—and saw their supreme challenge and purpose as the defeat of France.

In India and Asia, Richard saw French ambitions, French plots and expected to see French armies and navies everywhere, and although later his critics accused him of deliberately inventing a conspiracy to justify his personal ambitions, there was at the time justification for his view. In the 1780s the French had sent no less than ten naval expeditions to the East, mainly to chart the Red Sea route: they had strong points in Bengal, Madras, Batavia, Mauritius and Indo-China; there were French military adventurers in Central India among the Maratha states and in Hyderabad and Mysore. Bonaparte had just launched a diplomatic offensive in the Near and Middle East, and was preparing an attack from France across the Mediterranean into Egypt, which might well carry him into the Red Sea. In Britain's year of peril these facts were too numerous and ugly to be discounted.

In final conclave before he left London, Henry Dundas, the head of the India Board and soon to be War Minister, virtually in control of Indian policy and of the East India Court of Directors, had told Richard that in his view the right line was to hold a balance of power between the Indian states whilst concentrating on the elimination from the east of French influence and power.

At the Cape of Good Hope on the way out Richard had the good fortune to cross the path of William Kirkpatrick, lately

British Resident or Ambassador in Central India and Hyderabad, a man of twenty years' experience at the courts of the
Indian Princes, a gifted linguist, an eighteenth century Richard
Burton, than whom no one was more familiar with the true
state of Indian political affairs. Kirkpatrick told him that the
political leadership of India lay within Britain's grasp. If she
did not now reach out, she would miss a great chance and the
future of India would fall to be settled between on the one side
the infamous Tipu Sultan, ruler of Mysore who dominated the
south from his massive fortress of Seringapatam, and who was
threatening to eliminate the British in Madras, and on the
other side the Maratha Confederacy of Chiefs, whose pillaging
armies were the terror of Central India from the east to west
coasts and from the Ganges Valley in the north to Hyderabad
in the south. Moreover, in the light of India's history no one
could entirely discount the threats of the Afghans in the north-
west, where Zaman Shah and his army were striving to resolve
their own local troubles in order to enjoy the traditional inva-
sion of India like the Moguls and Nadir Shah before them.

Kirkpatrick's message, which chimed well in Richard's ears,
was that it was a time for decision, a time for greatness. But
Richard was fresh from London and only too keenly aware of
a fundamental dilemma. The fact was that for the East India
Company British India formed a deficit area, its costs of
administration and defence exceeding its revenues, and the
Company's profits arising not from the Indian but the China
trade. The conviction of the stockholders and directors of the
Company was that, since conquest had not been made to pay,
the Company should do no more than preserve its Indian
territory whilst retrenching its costs. An active minority even
felt that the time was ripe for the British, like other European
powers before them, to withdraw from Indian territory and
concentrate on trade. Therefore to persuade the London
Government and the Company's government into a forward
and probably expensive policy in India, Richard would need a
cast-iron case.

His anticipations sharpened by Kirkpatrick, Richard sailed
on to India—incidentally leaving behind a lovelorn Lady Anne,

the Governor's wife, who watched his ship until the sails dropped below the horizon. And Kirkpatrick, fired by the 'glorious little man' abandoned his trip to Europe and took the first ship back to Calcutta there to take up the especially created post of Political Secretary to the Governor-General.

Meanwhile Arthur had been looking around, seeking the means to set up his own future, travelling south to reconnoitre the likely campaign areas in the event of war with Tipu Sultan of Mysore, and making a cool, calculating appraisal of the British in Madras, one and all preoccupied in pillaging the revenues of the local ruler of Arcot; and disliking what he saw 'for the whole,' he said, 'is a system of job and corruption from beginning to end.'

With ambitions rising in his mind he still kept first things first and, when on 17 May 1798 Richard sailed up the river Hugli in the Governor-General's yacht and, 'dapper, aquiline and stately', stepped ashore at Calcutta, Arthur was there to greet him.

Then followed four hectic months, Richard taking stock of his Government and soon deciding that half of his executive council was useless and would have to go, and the three brothers urgently pooling their ideas. Arthur was set to work to write down virtually all he knew about men and affairs in India, displaying to advantage the long months of reading and reflection; and revelling in the prose of war, and soon displaying such a command of the genre as to put him in a class by himself. It was a phase in which he fast emerged as a 'full, ready and exact man'.

Almost as soon as Richard had taken over, news began to trickle through the Calcutta newspapers that Tipu Sultan, blindly feeling for allies inside and outside India, had been sending appeals for assistance against the British to Constantinople and Paris, and that the French Governor of Mauritius, M. Malartic, had openly welcomed Tipu's ambassadors, publicly announced an alliance and called for French volunteers to go to Mysore. In no doubt that this was a diplomatic and political blunder of the first magnitude, for it exposed Tipu's anti-

British policy while attracting no effective support, Richard thought the chance for a show-down was too good to be missed. But Arthur produced a cooling memorandum. There was little evidence of French forces actually reaching or likely to reach Mysore, but more important the brunt of any war would fall on Madras, which as he had seen was quite unready and unwilling. 'If it be possible to adopt a line of conduct which would not lead immediately to war', he wrote, 'it ought to be adopted in preference to that proposed in the conversations.'

Richard held his hand, but he sent sharp orders to General George Harris, the Madras Commander in Chief and Acting Governor, to put Madras on a war footing as soon as possible. Back came a prevaricating reply, for Harris, old and wily campaigner though he was, could not see how to divert the attention of his Madras Councillors from shaking 'the banyan tree' on their own behalf to producing the sinews of war for Richard. He prudently kept to generalities, but the Secretary to Government, Josiah Webbe, whom Arthur was later to praise as 'one of the most able and honest men I ever knew' was daring enough to spell out the reasons why Madras simply could not face war. 'Our Treasury is empty, our credit bankrupt.' The orders, he said, were impracticable, and if persisted with, the Governor-General would risk impeachment! Richard's anger flared. He was not thus to be flouted. Copiously fed from internal volcanoes, his language was a lava flow crushing Webbe and terrifying Harris. Nobody could doubt that a new and powerful force was at work in Calcutta; and that it would soon sweep through Madras.

Meanwhile, Kirkpatrick who had just joined the brothers in Calcutta, brought his first hand experience of Central India to bear, arguing that while the situation in Mysore and Madras was being allowed to mature, the British should strengthen their position in Hyderabad on Tipu's flank by offering to protect the Nizam's territories against raids from the Marathas in the north and from Tipu in the south, and persuading him to substitute British troops for his French military mercenaries whom he was known to fear. Under threat on all sides, on 11

September the Nizam, a weak, bewildered man, secretly accepted the offer, and five weeks later in a brilliantly engineered *coup*, a young Company officer, Captain John Malcolm disarmed and captured the French, about a hundred in number, and quickly established British control over the Nizam's army.

Even this *coup* did not lift morale in Madras. Re-armament was proceeding very slowly, and a new Governor, Lord Clive, son of the famous Clive of Arcot, had no sooner arrived than he appeared to succumb to the peace-at-any-price party.

Richard therefore sent Arthur to Madras with his regiment to stimulate the 'hum-drum Madrassers' and to bring Clive round to a proper viewpoint. But Clive was dull, not easily moved; his speech was slow, easily keeping pace with his thoughts, 'cast in the mould which Nature favours to obstruct the designs of bold and clever men'. 'How the devil did he get there?' angrily asked Richard. But Arthur, patient, cheerful, persuasive, closeted daily for several hours at a stretch with Clive, so won him round that Richard was soon pronouncing Clive 'a very sensible man'. In Richard's eyes it was Arthur's first triumph although Arthur felt privately that he had had to behave 'little better than a spy to achieve it'. Equally important was the good impression made by Arthur on the commander, Harris, and now that Richard was pouring money and supplies from Bengal into Madras, Harris did not hesitate to put Arthur in charge of the mobilisation area at Arcot from which any attack on Tipu would have to be launched.

But Madras still went in fear of Tipu. In fact, British intelligence services in Mysore were poor, and Tipu's monstrous cruelties to British prisoners had so mesmerised the Madras Councillors that they sought only to appease. Could they but have seen it, Tipu's empire and Tipu himself contained the seeds of dissolution. Inheriting from an able father an extensive, fertile country and an efficient army, Tipu at first possessed the power to control south India and smash the British in Madras. But he got lost between two unequal worlds; among Indian princes he was supreme but he was so eager to profit by Western science and philosophy, to follow the Revolutionary government of France in the view that everything is wrong and must be changed because it exists, that he could never hold to any one course. Constant innovation and change ruined his state and drove him on to ever monstrous tyranny, so that he had to seek safety in creating at his capital, Seringapatam, a massive fortress and army, and for private consolation turned to mysticism. There is in his papers later captured at Seringapatam a fascinating, personal account of his dreamlike trances, revealing that his days were increasingly spent in contemplation and the business of his government only slightly and fitfully attended to. From the evidence we can now see that he was politically a spent force, and his clumsy diplomatic game was childishly wayward. But the British in India, terrified by him, had yet to discern this.

Richard faced harsh choices. If he moved against Tipu, he ran the risk of exposing Bengal to Zaman Shah, already reported as being on the move towards Delhi. If he waited much longer, the Madras army in the field might find itself overtaken and marooned by the monsoon, which as Arthur warned him usually broke about 20 May in Mysore. But the timely arrival of a British fleet off Tipu's west coast encouraged Richard to take the risk of immediate war, so he at last formally demanded an explanation from Tipu of his anti-British policies. The reply was evasive. 'Being frequently disposed to make excursions and hunt,' said Tipu, 'I am accordingly proceeding on a hunting expedition,' with the casual addition that a British envoy 'slightly attended or unattended would not be unwelcome'. Richard's reponse was to sail south to Madras, personally to supervise the final war preparations and on 5 March to launch Harris and his army with orders to capture Tipu's fortress of Seringapatam.

Arthur had been a soldier for twelve years and had not yet taken part in a real battle. With the arrival of Harris and his staff in the mobilisation area, he had dropped from number one to number seven in seniority, so that it caused surprise and jealousy when Harris gave him command of a contingent of 20,000 troops from Hyderabad, now of course in alliance with the British.

Tipu, remote and fatalistic in his world of dreams, decided on a defensive, scorched-earth policy, hoping that the May monsoon would catch his enemy in the field. But Harris's cumbrous army and siege train rolled remorselessly up the easy eastern passes and across the Mysore plain at a steady average of five miles a day, with Richard maintaining more than adequate supplies from Madras, until in the first days of April it stood before the south western approaches to the great walls of Seringapatam, within which Tipu and his army of about 30,000 were entrenched, and began to probe the defences.

At this critical stage Arthur personally suffered a military defeat which could easily have ruined his career. It badly

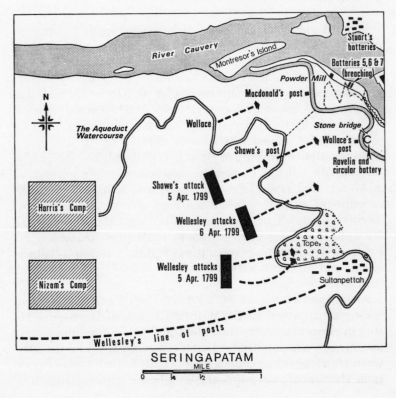

SERINGAPATAM
MILE
0   ¼   ½   1

He was never again personally to get so far forward in an attack as to lose control of his force as a whole. A man who is actively fighting, he wrote, cannot think to best advantage. Henceforward he took charge of his own intelligence services. Forty years later that unpleasant night lived in his memory and he could still draw a detailed sketch map in explanation. It was in fact the one recorded occasion in his mature life that he lost control. There is no sign here of the unmoving soldier of later years.

The way to Seringapatam now being clear the siege began in earnest, and within a month, with the huge, lion-hearted David Baird leading the assault, the fortress was stormed amidst scenes of great carnage and ferocity, Baird taking full revenge for those years which he had spent as Tipu's prisoner. Tipu himself died as he had lived, in futility and despair, to the last offering up elephants and goats for heavenly guidance and casually slaughtering his British prisoners as they were brought in, and himself finally falling victim to a pistol shot as he was being carried away wounded from an obscure mêlée. He died unmourned.

On the following morning, Arthur as the duty officer of the day, was instructed by Harris to take charge of the city as acting Governor with orders to quell the pillaging. Arthur reached Baird as he and his 'family' or staff were taking breakfast. 'General Baird, I am appointed to the command of Seringapatam and here is the order of General Harris.' Furious but ignoring him, the huge Scot rose 'Come, gentlemen, we have no longer any business here', but Arthur had the last word, 'Oh pray, finish your breakfast'. Baird rushed straight to Harris, 'Before the sweat was drying on my brow, I am superseded by an inferior officer.' But Harris brushed him aside saying that he was simply choosing the duty officer next on the roster. None of them, not even Harris perhaps realised that the man in command of Seringapatam on that day would become the permanent commandant.

With Tipu dead and the conquered city back to normal, Richard, who while waiting for news had suffered a nervous crisis and had to take to bed, joyfully got back into action. He had drawn up alternative master plans, one in the event of failure before Seringapatam, the other, which he now applied. He put in a Commission to administer the whole of Mysore. Under Harris, Arthur was to be the senior military officer; Henry, the only civilian, was to join him along with Colonel Barry Close, 'the ablest man in the diplomatic line in India'; with two secretaries, Thomas Munro, than whom no one knew more about land settlement, and the irrepressible John Malcolm, already famous for his work in Hyderabad. Almost immediately Harris saw fit to depart for Madras and England, there to enjoy his large share of the Seringapatam booty, and leaving Arthur as the senior in charge. It was a brilliant team which quickly took advantage of the Mysoreans' relief at the death of Tipu to settle the province and create it as a bastion of British power in the south.

This was a decisive phase. Astounded at the completeness of the British victory, the Marathas became aware of their own vulnerability. For the British there was no going back, withdrawal from India was unthinkable, and the struggle for the paramountcy of India had begun.

In the period immediately following, Arthur, in tracking down and suppressing the scattered remnants of Tipu's army, was drawn into the jungles and mountains of north Mysore, where in a series of minor campaigns he served his apprenticeship in the arts of guerilla warfare and began to confirm the reputation which his sure, decisive, fair management of Seringapatam had already created. But he was uneasily aware there was a dark side to the British triumph, that the completeness of the conquest of Mysore had let loose thousands of brigands, former soldiers, who were destroying the countryside. If the British conquest continued was this to be repeated on a wider, even more destructive scale throughout India?

Richard returned to Calcutta, where without Arthur or Henry to restrain him, the complete triumph in Hyderabad and Mysore went to his head. Already anticipating the conferment of at least an English marquisate, he had had his new coat of arms long since prepared, and meanwhile allowed his mind to soar over the prospects of bringing the whole of India under British control.

For Arthur about whose merits he could no longer seriously be in doubt there was meanwhile to be an independent command of some lucrative expedition or other, perhaps against French-controlled Batavia or Mauritius. Immediately, a military force of some 5,000 strong, along with naval units, was to be got together at Trincomalee in Ceylon, and Arthur was ordered to wind up his work in Mysore, to gather a headquarters staff of volunteers and take command as 'the most suitable officer available'. Delighted, believing that his hour for fortune if not fame had come, Arthur dropped everything and once in Ceylon settled down to a period of frenzied organisation, cut short, however, by direct orders from London that the Ceylon force should be sent to Egypt via the Red Sea as part of a British pincer movement against the French there.

At Calcutta, Richard's preferment of Arthur precipitated a first-class military row. Baird who had not forgotten the Sultanpettah failure nor forgiven his supersession, demanded his own appointment, and got the Bengal Commander-in-Chief to back him, and on the grounds that an enlarged expedition to Egypt ought to be in the hands of a general staff officer, which Arthur was not, forced Richard to agree that Baird should command, with Arthur as his deputy.

Meanwhile, aware of the need for speed in the Egyptian enterprise, Arthur, somewhat rashly considering his lack of staff rank, had set sail with his force for Bombay, so that when the unlucky Baird reached Ceylon his army had vanished and he had somewhat tamely to follow on to Bombay. It was not until actually at sea that Arthur had learnt of Baird's appointment. He could not contain his fury, 'I was at the top of the tree in this country . . . But this supersession has ruined all my prospects.' All his early bitterness against his brother flooded back. He had been wantonly treated, perhaps tricked, humiliated beyond recovery. What made things worse, Richard did not have the grace or brotherly feeling to explain why Baird had been preferred and had offered no apology, merely shifty letters of self-justification.

What was Arthur to do? As previously, when in a personal dilemma, emotionally upset, he became obsessional, he fell sick with fever, and in a weakened condition caught the Malabar itch, a kind of ringworm. So the expedition sailed under Baird without him; and his treatment, nitric acid baths, proving worse than the disease, he suffered a relapse, so that the ship which he later intended to travel on, also had to depart without him— as it happened never to be seen again.

So Arthur had to seek the grace of Lord Clive in Madras and humbly ask to be allowed to return to his Regiment, but Clive sensibly posted him back to his command in Mysore.

In Calcutta, Richard too, had tasted bitterness. London had not gone into the anticipated ecstasies over his Mysore triumphs. Only an Irish marquisate had been conferred on him. It was the worst insult: 'Nothing short of an English marquisate,' he wrote, 'granted instantly, can satisfy me . . . or save my life. My fame in India is gone, and with it all prospect of happiness in this life.' He meant it, too, for he gave total public service and expected in return the highest public rewards! Beside himself with rage and mortification, he fell from the skies to earth, sulked in his study, refused to deal with any business for almost six months, and finally suffered a nervous collapse, out of which he was only drawn by the devotion of his young staff.

From London, Pitt's cabinet, borne on a rising tide of European successes against France, pressed Richard once for all to expel French influence from India and the East. For Richard this was tantamount to suggesting that he should bring the Maratha chiefs under control, for they were the harbourers of European military adventurers, many of them being French. Anyway, this marched with his own ideas, and offered him the chance of showing the King and his ministers in London what he was capable of. The dukedom might yet be grasped.

But he was now alone in Government House, as it were confined by absolute power. Kirkpatrick had gone, Henry was on his way to London to present Richard's case on Mysore, and Arthur was hostile, indeed had ceased entirely to write to him; and when challenged on this, insultingly answered that at least he could be sure of an answer from Richard's secretary. Richard had no one with him who knew the Marathas at first hand. His own yardstick was European, with a framework of national states, well-defined frontiers, structured governments and ministries: he spoke of the Maratha 'Empire' and its frontiers as if it was unitary, with one overlord, the Peshwa, Baji Rao, and the Maratha 'Government' and 'Constitution' as if it was a firm political organisation: but all this was misconceived and it proved to be his undoing.

The Maratha Confederacy was in fact a loose political grouping of five great princely families, Sindhia, Holkar, Baroda, Berar, and the Peshwa, the last being by far the weakest though nominally recognised as the head, treaties for example often being signed by them in his name. Richard took it for granted that the Peshwa *was* the paramount Maratha authority, and that if he could control him, he could control all. It was true that the Marathas themselves had an underlying unity; they were Hindu, with their own language and way of life, physically small and hardy, with a flair for guerilla warfare. Their writ ran with the shadow of their horses, and they ranged from Delhi in the north to Hyderabad in the south, and from coast to coast, a thousand miles each way. But they were uninterested in the world outside; totally ignorant of the Company and Britain, their intelligence service was pathetic and their maps utter fantasies. As with Tipu, this was a clash of two worlds of differing ethics and views and habits of life. The one thing that they had in common with the British in India was that they liked fighting!

For some years the two strongest chiefs in fact, Sindhia and Holkar, had kept Maratha affairs on the boil by competing to control the Peshwa, and if necessary to keep him prisoner. At this period, Sindhia was temporarily in control, but in October 1802 Holkar defeated him near Poona, and threatened to carry off the Peshwa. The latter was a young man of twenty-five, superficially personable, with an ingratiating presence, eloquent and apparently eager to please, yet an intriguer to the bone. 'To trust none, and to deceive all was the game he invariably played.' With those in his power he was faithless, cowardly and cruel beyond belief. For revenge on Holkar he captured his brother, and gleefully watched from a window while the victim was flogged and then tied to the foot of an elephant, slowly to be trodden to death. When both Sindhia and Holkar threatened to take and imprison him, he appealed for help to the Governor-General.

This was the chance Richard had been waiting for. He had already sent his best diplomats, Kirkpatrick and Barry Close. to persuade the Peshwa of the merits of a subsidiary alliance. Now 'this crisis of affairs,' he said, 'affords the most favourable opportunity for the complete establishment of the interests of the British power in the Maratha empire, without the hazard of involving us in a contest with any party.'

At Bassein on the coast near Bombay, where the Peshwa had fled for safety, Barry Close persuaded him to accept a treaty—named after Bassein—providing for his restoration and main-tenance at Poona with a British subsidiary force, on condition that all Frenchmen were expelled from Maratha country, and the Governor-General was given the right of arbitration in his relations with all other Indian powers. If in the Maratha context he thought this was a prescription for peace, Richard was deluding himself. Close, who knew better, had no illusions. A subsidiary alliance with the nominal head of the Marathas was a challenge to all the Maratha chiefs, and interference in their quarrels was bound to be seen as aggressive.

Richard's immediate aim was to restore the Peshwa safely to Poona; which could only be done from the secure British position in the south. As good fortune had it, Arthur's promo-tion as Major-General had just come through, and the newly appointed and discerning Madras Commander-in-Chief, General James Stuart, gave him a temporary Madras appointment on the staff, and fell in with Richard's proposal that on the north Mysore border at Hurryhur, Arthur should organise the army of the south to be ready to move into Maratha-land. Ignoring London's agitated accusations of excessive expenditure, Richard committed the unforgivable crime in the eyes of the Directors of extracting large quantities of bullion from the Company's China fleet and lavishly supplied Arthur, ordering him to restore the Peshwa to Poona, 500 miles distance in the heart of the Maratha country, in effect without involving the Company in war. It was a tall order.

Nearly 15,000 troops were mobilised, 2,700 being European, mainly cavalry with artillery, the rest being sepoy infantry, and a second army of nearly 9,000 was gathered under Colonel Stevenson, a much older man than Arthur; and to these were added a miscellaneous, somewhat inefficient force from Hyderabad, about 15,000 men in all. In due course these armies and support troops grew to 50,000 in total size.

As his personal political adviser, Arthur was given John Malcolm, who after his great *coup* in Hyderabad and service in Mysore had become Richard's political trouble shooter; and they were of course to work with Barry Close, now Political Resident with Sindhia, rightly said to be the man with the sharpest eyes and mind in India. As a team, Arthur Wellesley, Malcolm and Close had already proved themselves in Mysore. John Malcolm, or 'Boy' Malcolm as he was happily called, brought a special, lighthearted flavour to Arthur's rather sombre, often war-weary camp. Around him there was always a buzz of lively conversation, an unfailing flow of animal spirits. He got on well with everyone, whether Indian, British, Persian or Afghan. With his amusingly squeaky voice, he was a constant source of fun, always arriving in camp with 'a brisk explosion of jokes', and not surprisingly became Arthur's best and life-long friend.

The campaign which Arthur conducted in Maratha country made his military reputation. Culminating in the battle of Assaye it was revolutionary in concept, quite transforming the style of war in India and permanently enriching the art of guerilla fighting. In this his previous experience in clearing and settling Mysore formed the essential preparation. The prime factors were the distances involved in rough, often arid, sometimes jungly country scored by deep river beds, often impassable in the monsoon, and the fact that an Indo-British army, far from its base in Mysore, was bound to carry for its European troops salt beef, biscuit, arrack or rum, and medicines as well as ammunition, and tents, and would therefore be heavily laden.

To appreciate fully the revolutionary character of the changes which he introduced we have only to recall the progress and style of Harris's army on its way to Seringapatam.

That army marched in a vast rectangle six miles long, three miles wide: inside went everything, a moving city, with 150,000 camp followers, men, women and children, 60,000 of the Company's bullocks, camels, elephants, horses, carriages, battering train and arsenal, and double that number of animals belonging to individuals. Arthur described it as 'a multitude in motion which covered about eighteen square miles' and moved five miles a day.

His own strategy was based on the ability to out-march a mobile enemy and to keep his troops supplied. He had already perfected a supply system through Indian brinjarries, or merchants, who moved their bazaars and transport with the army, and since Richard kept him plentifully supplied with bullion, he proposed to pay as he went for all fodder which the countryside could furnish. But his men and animals from the south could not live on the coarse grain which satisfied the Maratha and his horse, so a system of protected convoys was organised—each consisting of six to eight thousand bullocks, loaded with 120 lbs to each bullock, travelling eight miles a day. All supplies were pre-packed for loading in four gallon kegs for liquids or 72 lb gunny bags for solids. Where his men could march, there his pack bullocks could follow. 'Where I had bullocks, I had men, and with men, I could win.' He also had a group of female elephants, to help with the artillery, each of which needed daily 40 lbs of rice, a pound of butter, and date palm juice, and 40 large coconut palm leaves. To ensure the safe conduct of convoys through jungles he hired gangs of coolies to clear by hand up to 200 yards each side of the route.

From Tipu's Mysore stud fine heavy white bullocks had been bred to draw the carriages and guns, twelve bullocks to each six pounder gun, and so successfully that they could actually outmarch the infantry. Officers' private vehicles were prohibited, the sole exception being 'a tumbril for the commander's papers'. Operating against irregular, light forces of cavalry, it was also essential to have an effective system of intelligence. No money was spared on this, and for speed both camels, which could travel at 15 m.p.h., and relays of runners were employed, and lavishly paid. His personal staff was kept small, no more than eight officers in a force of 50,000, and Arthur held direct control of intelligence.

Quickly and if possible peacefully to get to Poona some 500 miles away, Arthur decided to by-pass all Maratha forts, and by paying his way and scrupulously protecting the villagers, much to their astonishment for this was not their previous experience of armies, he succeeded. Averaging twenty miles a day between dawn and noon, the marching period, and making a final cavalry dash of sixty miles through the night, he surprised Sindhia's troops into evacuating Poona without a fight; and on 13 May duly reinstated the Peshwa.

If there had been any doubts in the minds of the Maratha leaders on the implications of the Treaty of Bassein, Arthur's precipitate arrival in Poona must have dispelled them; and if Arthur had any doubts on the nature of the British commitment, they were expelled by the immediate efforts of the Peshwa to involve the British in war with all of his former enemies. But Arthur had completed his military mission successfully, and in Richard's sanguine expectation, a conclusive, political phase of intricate negotiation would immediately follow. Communication, however, between Richard in Government House, Calcutta, and Arthur's camp was slow, some forty or more days being required for a reply. Richard therefore boldly gave Arthur supreme command in the south, both military and political, in dealing with the Marathas; essentially, therefore he held the power to make war or peace.

The first need was to placate Sindhia, who rejected the idea of a subsidiary alliance, and threatened to bring about a coalition of Maratha chiefs to expel the British. On being asked to declare his objections to the Treaty of Bassein, Sindhia would not answer, but instead began moving his cavalry for a raid into Hyderabad. When he failed to halt his movements or give any reply, Arthur declared war.

To move north from Poona against the main force of Sindhia and his ally, Berar, meant operating in wild country, intersected by deep river crossings, which quickly became perilous in the monsoon. Arthur's first concern therefore was to secure the line of the river crossings, and at each point to maintain and guard a supply of basket boats. This done he was ready 'to cross the Godaveri river and bring the enemy to action'. But he was up against a tough, fast-moving enemy, whose wants, both man and beast, were of the slightest, and who allowed himself only one luxury, the courtesan; and the women in fact fought and pillaged as pitilessly as the men.

Arthur's actual expeditionary force was small—some 2,200 European and 5,000 sepoy troops, with about 6,200 light horse from his Mysore and Maratha allies. But every man was a volunteer and of high quality, and many of the Europeans had served in the field for more than ten years. They had proved their mobility and stamina. But could they fight? Arthur had proved his logistic capacity and flair for guerilla warfare, but could he win a set battle and destroy the enemy's main force, and will to continue the war?

The armies manoeuvred for position. Sindhia with his light cavalry wished to move south for a pillaging raid into Hyderabad, but could not get sufficiently clear of Arthur's force, which in the pursuit crossed the Godaveri three times in as many weeks. Arthur now brought northwards Colonel Stevenson with a small army, so that between them they might corner Sindhia, and the latter, giving up his idea of a dash into Hyderabad, countered by bringing south his famous Regular Battalions of Infantry, which regardless of expense had been raised and equipped and were trained and led by European adventurers, mainly British and French, though their commander, Pohlmann, was German. Their equipment was in no way inferior to the British, but they had never met the British in battle and no one knew their real fighting quality. One of Arthur's men, who had watched them drill, estimated their number at 20,000, and praised them, warning Arthur 'Their infantry and guns will surprise you'. Arthur's practical conclusion, however, was that by bringing up his massive force of infantry, Sindhia had sacrificed the Maratha's main advantage of mobility, and might now be brought to battle. The more infantry he had, the more vulnerable he was.

At this juncture, Arthur's camp was no more than a mile from that of Stevenson. At a meeting on 21 September Arthur re-emphasised his strategy—'Dash at the first fellows that make their appearance and the campaign will be our own. A long, defensive war will ruin us'. Sindhia's forces were known to be only thirty miles away at the end of a line of hills. The problem was how to surprise and bring them to battle. Arthur and Stevenson agreed to march one each side of the line of hills, in order to make sure that Sindhia did not slip away through any of the passes, and three days later at the further end to join forces and give battle.

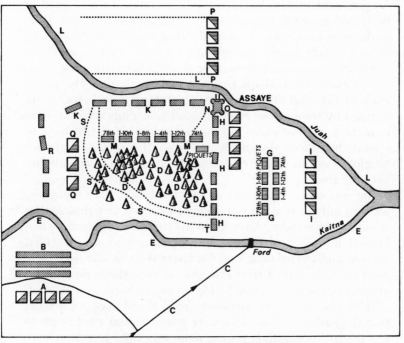

SKETCH PLAN OF BATTLE OF ASSAYE
From Mr Elphinstone's Sketch

On 23 September Arthur's army covered fourteen miles before noon, and halted in the belief that Sindhia's forces were still ten miles away, but a group of grain merchants, intercepted on their way to Sindhia's camp, revealed that they were much nearer. Arthur had to make an immediate decision. He was greatly outnumbered but if he waited for Stevenson, he would lose touch with Sindhia, so resting his infantry in camp, he rode with two cavalry regiments across and up the long treeless slope, and leaving them just below the sky-line went forward to a low ridge above the Kaitna river.

It was a spectacular scene. Before him was Sindhia's whole army and camp, spread over six miles; with the massed Regular Battalions beyond the river in front of the fortified village of Assaye, between the Kaitna and Juah rivers. They seemed to be breaking camp, perhaps on learning of his approach. If he could attack at once, he would catch them off-balance, and although their numerical superiority was enormous, 40,000 to 5,800, he discounted this because in a confined area only their front formations, perhaps 10,000, could be effective. He at once made up his mind to fight and galloped straight back, fruitlessly pursued by some of the enemy. Leaving one infantry battalion to make a fortified camp, on the chance that he might have to retreat, he moved the cavalry to cover the Kaitna, and then sought to get his infantry across the front of the enemy and over the river.

But was there a ford and where? His local guides said there was but only in front of the enemy's infantry, but that Arthur rejected as too risky. Anyway to his right downstream he had himself noticed two villages on opposite sides of the river, Waroor and Peepalgoun, and his inspired guess was that there must be some sort of river-crossing between them. So with his infantry in column covered by his cavalry he headed for Waroor.

With his orderly he anxiously rode ahead, saw with relief that the banks on both sides were passable, and went down to test the river's depth. It proved to be only three feet deep, with a firm bottom; and the infantry were waved on. They were now under artillery fire from across the river, a cannon ball removing the head from Arthur's orderly, the frantic horse plunging about with the body still wedged in the saddle.

Unable to see over the rising ground beyond the river, Arthur guessed that there was insufficient space between the two rivers to deploy his army in a single line, so he ordered double lines, with the cavalry sent right across to cover the far flank. But as he rode up the bank he saw that his guess was wrong, that Assaye village, bristling with guns, was nearly a mile away. Moreover, Sindhia's Regular Battalions had surprised him by changing front 'in the most steady manner', and were moving into line to cover the whole area between the two rivers, the Kaitna and the Juah, with their hinge on Assaye itself. On his way back to the ford he therefore warned his cavalry commander, Maxwell, to cover the right flank but to keep well away from Assaye.

By this time his own infantry had crossed the river and were turning leftwards into line, the 78th Highland kilted regiment nearest the Kaitna, and as they swung into line Arthur joined them, at once ordering a frontal assault. The charge was ferociously made, clearing 900 yards of the line. The four sepoy battalions to the right went out of control, but the 78th reformed and calmly fought off a Maratha cavalry counter charge. In the attack Arthur's bay horse was killed and he remounted on his favourite grey Arab, Diomed. Towards the centre of the line one of his infantry commanders, Colonel Orrock, as he was bringing his men into line made a tragic mistake and went off at an angle towards Assaye village so coming under terrible fire. The 74th King's Regiment went to their aid, but had to go to ground in the open; there to be attacked by Maratha horse, and only saved by forming a square.

Seeing this Maxwell ordered his cavalry to charge, cleared the area before Assaye, took the enemy guns and destroyed a regiment beyond, but his men went out of control, disappearing across the Juah river, and over the far bank.

Meanwhile, Sindhia's Regular Battalions had fallen back and formed again along the Juah, and Maxwell, who had somehow re-gathered part of his cavalry and got back over the river, was ordered to clear them, but his attack swung away before their fire. Arthur, now on his third horse, Diomed having been piked and lost[1], brought forward the 78th again, but Sindhia's infantry had had enough, and fled across the Juah, abandoning their guns and equipment, leaving the battlefield completely in Arthur's hands. Every Maratha gun—102 of them—and ammunition wagon was captured. But no pursuit was possible because the army was exhausted, having been marching and fighting since dawn. They slept where they were. Arthur spent the night on straw in a farmyard between a dead officer on one side and one with a leg shot off; and in broken, disturbed nightmares dreamed that he alone survived, that all of his companions had been killed.

Young Mountstuart Elphinstone, who was there, described the night scene:

There was a Roman Emperor who said he liked the smell of a dead enemy. If he did he was singular in his taste. We are horribly perfumed with such a smell as he liked, but I would rather smell a living enemy. I went yesterday evening to the field of battle. It was a dark, cloudy evening. I rode by myself, and saw *plurima mortis imago*. Some of the dead are withered, their features still remaining, but their faces blackened to the colour of coal, others still swollen and blistered. The Persian I mentioned was perfect everywhere, and has his great quilted coat on; but his face had fallen or been eaten off, and his naked skull stared out . . . Kites and adjutants, larger than the Calcutta ones, were feeding on the bodies, and dogs were feasting in some places, and in others howling all over the plain. I saw a black dog tearing, in a furious way, great pieces of flesh from a dead man, looking fiercely, and not regarding me. I thought the group horrible and sublime.

But Arthur and his army had proved that they could win a set battle[2].

British losses were severe, nearly 1,600 out of 5,800. Most were

---

[1] Arthur mourned Diomed, but some months later John Malcolm in Bombay saw a Maratha leading the sick, thin Diomed to the horse market, and was able to buy him for Rs 200, duly restoring the horse, when recovered, to the delighted Arthur.

[2] In the calculated way that Arthur set up and fought this battle, I have been reminded of the similar circumstances in which T. E. Lawrence did exactly the same. Lawrence's account occurs in chapter x of *The Seven Pillars of Wisdom*.

in the 74th Regiment which lost 60 per cent of its men actually engaged. Over the whole army it averaged 27 per cent. Only Waterloo of all Arthur's battles ever approached anything like that.

As a rehearsal for Waterloo, Assaye had an uncanny similarity. The battle areas were confined, Assaye being no more than one mile square as compared with Waterloo's three square miles, with large forces to be handled and little room for manoeuvre, so that hard pounding was the order of the day. Each witnessed uncontrollable charges of cavalry, the forming of squares and the massing of guns. Above all there was the personal rôle of the commander on the battlefield itself:

He was everywhere . . . the eye could turn in no direction that it did not perceive him, either at hand or at a distance; galloping to charge the enemy, or darting across the field to issue orders. Every ball also . . . seemed fired, and every gun aimed at him . . . But he suffered nothing to check or engage him . . . his entire, concentrated attention, exclusive aim, and intense thought were devoted impartially, imperturbably and grandly to the whole.

This was said of him at Waterloo and is just as true of Assaye.

Military critics have faulted Wellington in his European campaigns for a lack of audacity and offensive flair. Assaye showed the opposite. He had preached the offensive, and when the chance came, he took it. Years later, long after Waterloo, a friend asked him, 'What was the best you ever did in the way of fighting?' 'Assaye', replied Arthur sombrely; and said not another word. He might well be silent for Assaye had taught him the high cost of impulsive assault and he never again, until Waterloo, indulged in it.

After Assaye, victory followed victory. Richard's brilliantly conceived and executed strategic plan succeeded in trapping Sindhia between General Lake's forces in the north and Arthur's army to the south, and when it seemed certain that Sindhia would even lose his central and favourite fortress of Gwalior, he sued for peace.

It fell to Arthur and Malcolm to settle the terms. By now, unlike Richard, they pretty well understood the true nature of the Maratha Confederacy; its ramshackle organisation and absence of boundaries: its titular head, the Peshwa, a mere cipher not a King, its chiefs devoid of rational policies, their shifting alliances dependent on momentary fears of loss or hope of gain. To impose a subsidiary alliance, to insert the Company's forces and to disband their armies would be to alienate the Chiefs and set loose a horde of freebooters. Rather than see this happen, Arthur would have drawn the Company's frontier and, by a policy of divide and rule, maintained a balance of power, leaving them alone as much as possible. Richard, however, could not see any merit in this. He would deal with the Maratha chiefs as he had dealt with Tipu, and either destroy or control them. If the latter, he must have a subsidiary treaty, so Arthur, protesting against this 'demon of ambition', reluctantly gave way and through Malcolm imposed subsidiary treaties on Sindhia, Berar, and Baroda.

But Sindhia, as Arthur and Malcolm well knew, had only agreed to peace to save his central fortress of Gwalior, and therefore to avoid humiliating him had made no reference to it in their treaty. Sindhia's Minister, Wattel Punt, well knowing that the fortress had already been included in previous treaties, kept silent. Richard, fully aware that he had legality on his side, demanded the cession of Gwalior, meanwhile ranting against Arthur's supposed weakness—'The question is whether General Wellesley has not made a worse peace than Wattel Punt', and would not sign until he got his way[3].

Richard, now fundamentally a sick man, hovering permanently on the edge of breakdown, exasperated because the other Maratha Chief, Holkar, had at last decided to take a hand in the war, feared that London would recall him in disgrace, and that Arthur was giving to the public the disastrous impression 'that the right is with Sindhia and that it has been trampled

---

[3] Wattel Punt incidentally for his inscrutable manner was nicknamed Old Brag—Old Poker Face, by Malcolm. Arthur had great respect for his ability and in later years when Malcolm happened to be asking what Arthur thought of Talleyrand, he replied, 'A good deal like Old Brag, but not so clever'.

upon by Lord Wellesley'. In a note, Malcolm argued 'God knows my attention has been exclusively directed to one object, the promotion of the public interests', and got the same note back from Richard annotated, 'Mr. Malcolm's duty is to obey my orders . . . I will look after the public interests'. For Arthur this indication of ruthlessness was shocking, but beyond this, there was for him an even greater question at issue, 'The system of moderation and conciliation by which, whether it be right or wrong, I made the treaties of peace . . . is now given up'. His own principle was plain. 'I would sacrifice Gwalior or every frontier of India ten times over, in order to preserve our credit for scrupulous good faith.' If Richard had his way, he would destroy Indian leadership and Indian society with it.

In the south, the monsoon had failed leaving Arthur's army without fodder so that it was literally high and dry, and unable to move against Holkar. So Richard summoned Arthur to Calcutta, taking it for granted that the army commander in the north, General Lake, would find a rôle for him. But Lake, unwilling to share his own anticipated laurels of victory, did not respond, foolishly as it happened because he shortly suffered two severe defeats, which finally put an end to Richard's hopes of a quick triumph.

But Arthur had been put in an impossible position. Slighted by Lake, his acting rank of Major-General still unconfirmed by London, he could any day have been superseded by an inferior in service. He found Richard personally quite intolerable, and no doubt because of Holkar's victories, suffering from one of his strange spells of idleness and lethargy. He could not see the necessity of staying 'in order to settle affairs which, if I had been permitted, I should have settled long ago.' He had been in India for seven and a half years and was now thirty-five. 'I have served as long in India as any man ought.' As on previous occasions when caught in this kind of personal crisis he fell ill 'with a slow fever', 'grew lean', and 'wasted away daily'. 'My strength failed, which had always before held out.' Early in 1805 he sailed for Europe.

In conclusion, I come back to the view which I expressed at

35

the start that Richard and Arthur stood for two different philosophies of conquest and government.

Before the period and achievement of these men in India—the three Wellesleys, Thomas Munro, John Malcolm, Mountstuart Elphinstone, Barry Close—it was just conceivable that Britain, like France, could have withdrawn: after them it was out of the question; the die was cast. Britain was paramount and set on the perilous, imperial venture from which she has only recently emerged.

Apart from the high sense of adventure, 'the kingdom and the glory', largely imparted by Richard Wellesley and shared by all, Arthur and his colleagues took a very different view from Richard, the Governor-General. Arthur and his group showed a remarkable identity of understanding and purpose and nobility of behaviour. No other period threw up so many who were so uniformly great. How did this come about? Their origins could scarcely have been more diverse. They were all young, several reaching India when scarcely out of childhood. India was their education. They were veterans at thirty, with a cool nerve, long courage; and as Elphinstone said, of high spirit, 'at war with all the world and never suffering in the contest'.

All without question accepted Arthur's leadership. Like him all had faced early personal difficulties which they overcame successfully. They had found and proved themselves. Sometimes alone, sometimes as a group, they sojourned in the wilderness; in camp together for months on end in a vivid land where Alexander had marched they read and argued their way —through Plutarch, the Stoics, Thucydides—into a sense of history on the one hand and into an almost Confucian-like tolerance on the other. Above all aware of their own minuteness among Indian society, they came to the conclusion that a power which could not work through the existing forms of that society must prove destructive, 'a fearful experiment . . . so calculated as to flatten the whole surface of society'. Between Government and the peasant there would be nothing. As the night follows day, despotism would come.

Impressed by the varieties rather than the uniformity of

human nature, they were against sweeping innovation or regulation; they preferred organic growth to social engineering; social peace to impartial social justice. 'When I read, as I sometimes do,' said Malcolm, 'of a measure by which a large province has been suddenly improved, or a race of semi-barbarians civilised almost to Quakerism, I throw away the book'. They were free from the conviction that they represented civilization at war with savagery.

But Richard, the Governor-General, was different, nearer in spirit to those British successors who came to dominate India: the men of the Punjab and the Mutiny, the Rationalists and Evangelicals among others, who, taking their cue from prevailing sociological thinking in Britain, assumed that human nature was everywhere uniform, men mentally everywhere the same, and progress inevitable. Asia was Europe writ large. This was the world not as it *was*, but as they *wished* it to be. It was a view and a policy which produced the empire of Curzon's day, and, persisting into our own time brought Britain in the East and in Europe to near disaster. If we seek a guiding light today we would do well to look back to the earlier, almost forgotten picture.

But let me round off my own story with a brief postscript on a lighter note.

On leaving India perhaps the best indication of Arthur's state of mind, or should I say heart, was his choice of reading for the voyage home. On the way out, as we have seen, he had taken a library which would have done honour to the non-fiction section of a public institution. He came back with a collection which would have graced the shelves of a young ladies' circulating library. He had chosen twenty-six novels: *Illicit Love* and *Filial Indiscretion* in one volume each, *Lessons for Lovers* in two volumes, *Love at First Sight* in five volumes; and as gifts ten pairs of ladies' Oriental sandals. Evidently his Indian saga was not quite complete; the image of wasted youth not quite restored. The jigsaw lacked one piece. Safely home, the question was would Kitty Pakenham, whom he had not had direct contact with, or seen, for seven years, would she have him? She would; and he was promptly at the altar, later to add, as he so often did, the perfect verdict—'Would you have believed that anyone could be such a *damned* fool!'

CREIGHTON LECTURES IN HISTORY

50p net   0 485 14120

CREIGHTON LECTURES IN HISTORY

50p net   0 485 14120